T5-AFP-105

I WANT TO KNOW ABOUT . . . . ©.
Volume 15
Section A

SPIDERS

By Illa Podendorf

Pictures by Betsy Warren

CHILDRENS PRESS, CHICAGO

GROLIER ENTERPRISES, CANADA

CONTENTS

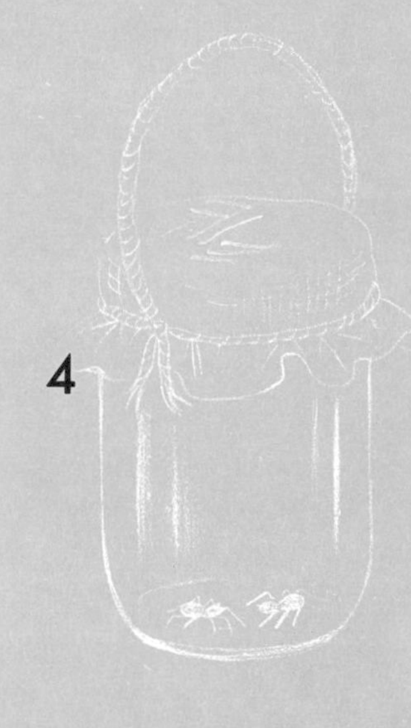

Printed in the United States of America.

WHAT ARE SPIDERS?

On these pages are pictures of six different kinds of animals.

Each of them belongs to a different group of animals.

Can you tell which one is the spider?

You know that the bird, the fish, the cat, the earthworm are not spiders. You probably know that the bee is an insect. Then the animal with the plump body and long legs must be a spider. It is in a web, too. That makes one think that it might be a spider.

TUNNEL WEB (GRASS SPIDER)

Here a spider and an insect are both in a web.

You cannot be sure that an animal is a spider just because it is in a spider web.

Here are pictures of another kind of spider and another kind of insect. You know that the butterfly is an insect.

Let's find out what spiders have that makes them different than insects.

MONARCH BUTTERFLY

FISHER SPIDER

Look carefully at these five different kinds of spiders.

How are they alike?

How many legs do they have?

All spiders have eight legs.

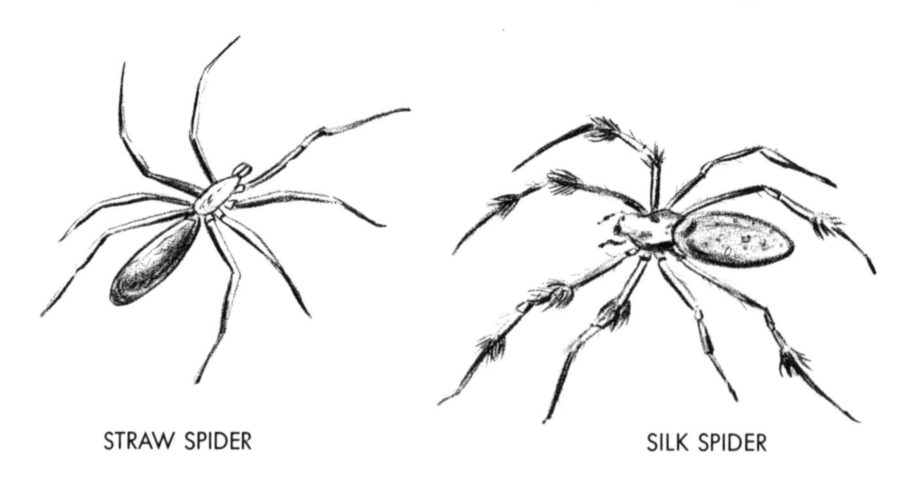

ANT

WASP

Here are pictures of three kinds of insects.

Each insect has six legs.

All insects have six legs.

MOTH

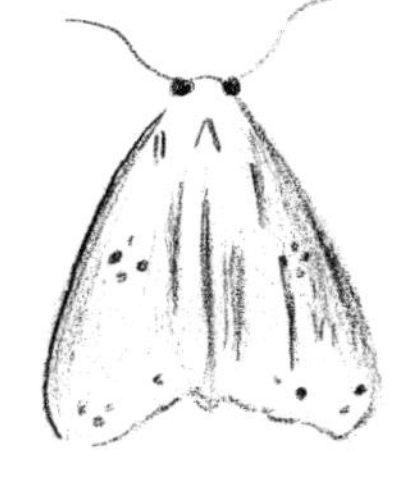

(WITH WINGS CLOSED)

Look at the pictures on page 10.
All spiders have plump bodies.
Spider bodies are in two parts, the head and the plump part — the *abdomen.*

Look at the pictures on page 11.
Insect bodies are not so plump as spider bodies. Insects have a body part between the head and the abdomen. It is called the *thorax.* The legs are all fastened to it.

You can see also that no spider has feelers.

All insects have feelers.

This is another difference between spiders and insects.

KATYDID

It is easy to see the
six legs and the feelers
on a katydid, an insect.

ARE ALL SPIDERS ALIKE?

Here are pictures of three kinds of spiders. They all have eight legs and plump bodies.

They do not have feelers.

It is interesting to know that most spiders have eight eyes.

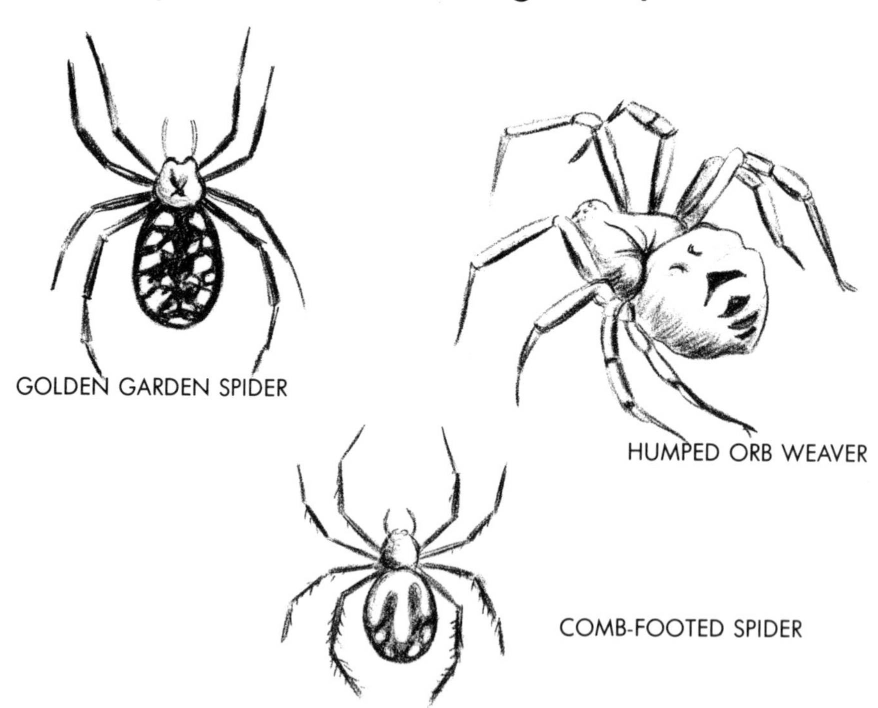

TRIANGLE SPIDER

Each kind of spider has a name of its own.

Spiders are alike in some ways.

They are different from each other, too.

Some spiders are bigger than others.

TARANTULA

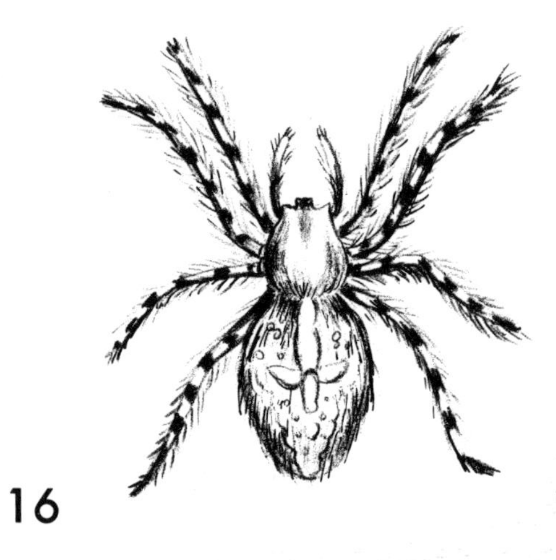

COMMON CROSS SPIDER

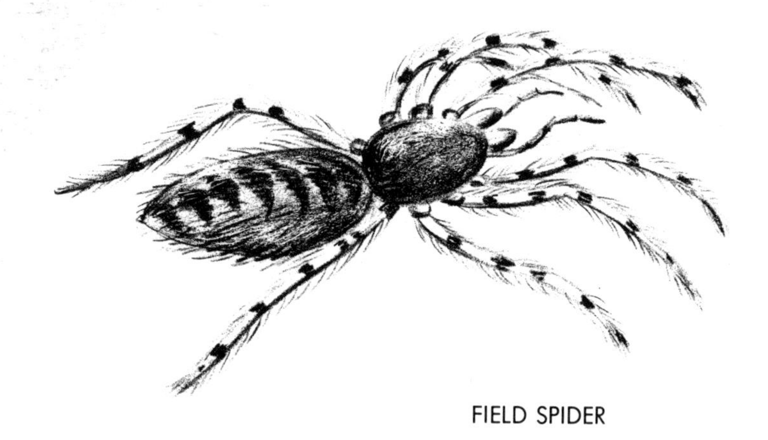

FIELD SPIDER

Some spiders have fuzzy bodies and others do not.

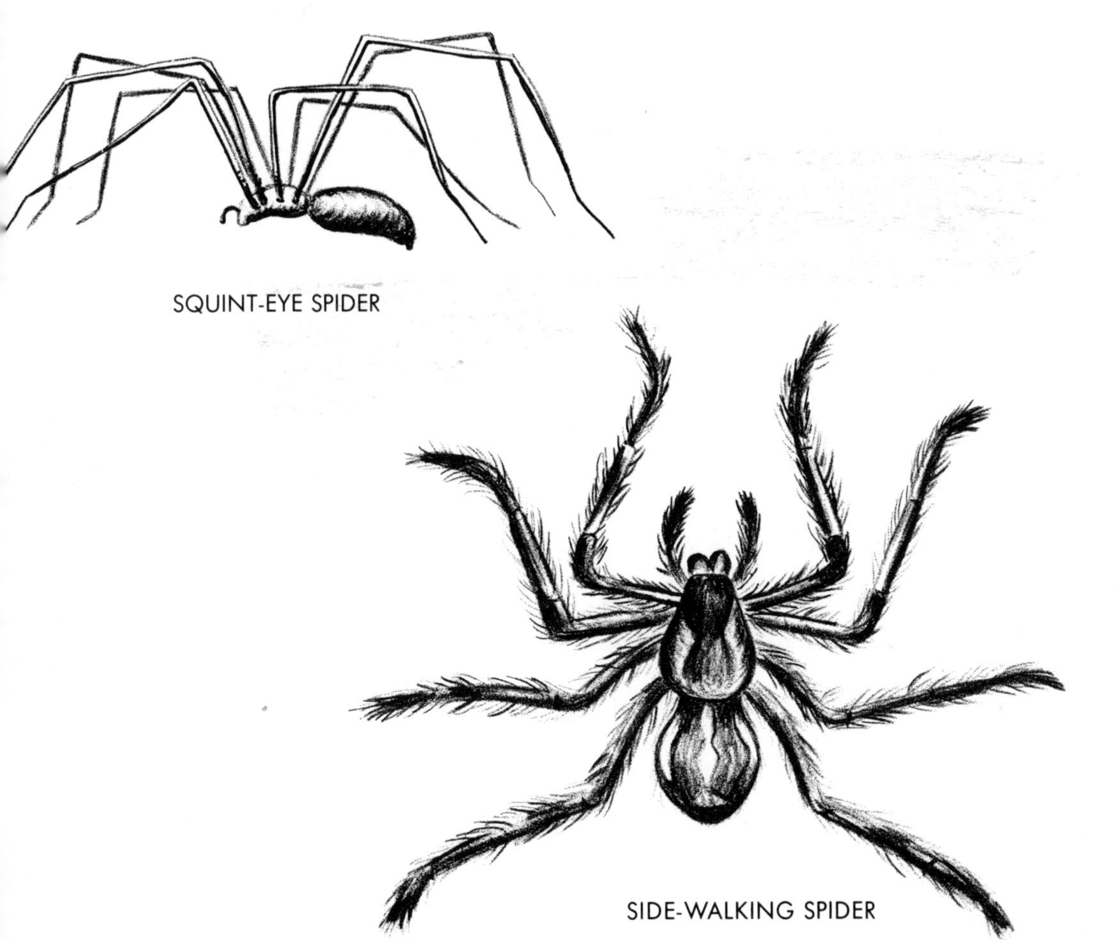

SQUINT-EYE SPIDER

SIDE-WALKING SPIDER

Some spiders have longer legs than others.

WHERE DO SPIDERS LIVE?

Spiders live in different kinds of places.

Some live where it is hot.
Some live where it is cold.
Some live where it is wet, and some live where it is dry.

Some live in houses.
Some live in gardens.

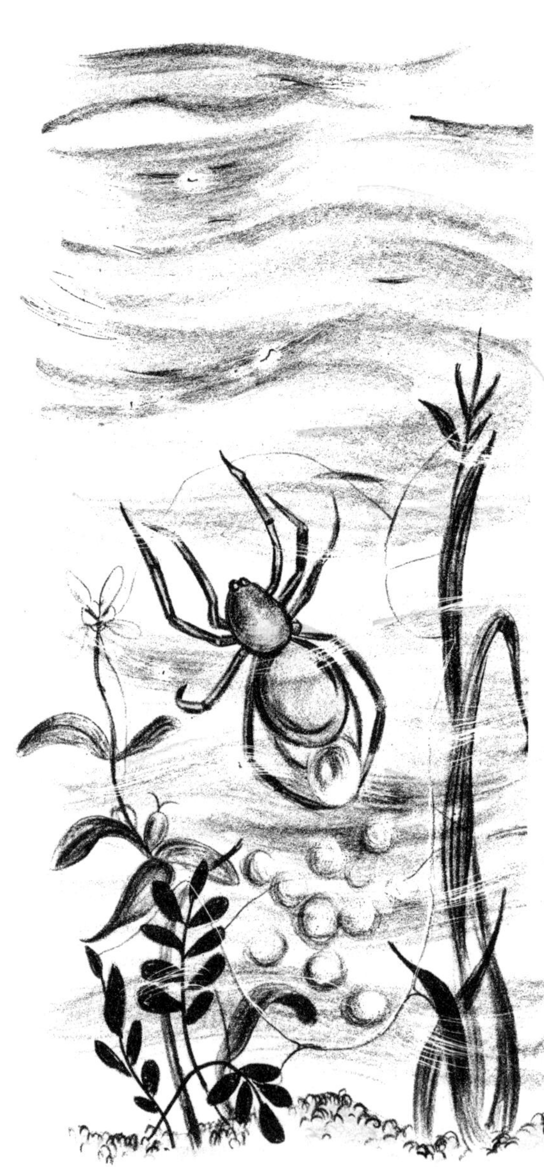

Some spiders live in water. They come to the top of the water for air.

Bubbles of air collect on hairs of their legs. They take this air down and store it at the bottom of the water. When the air is gone, they come up for more bubbles of it.

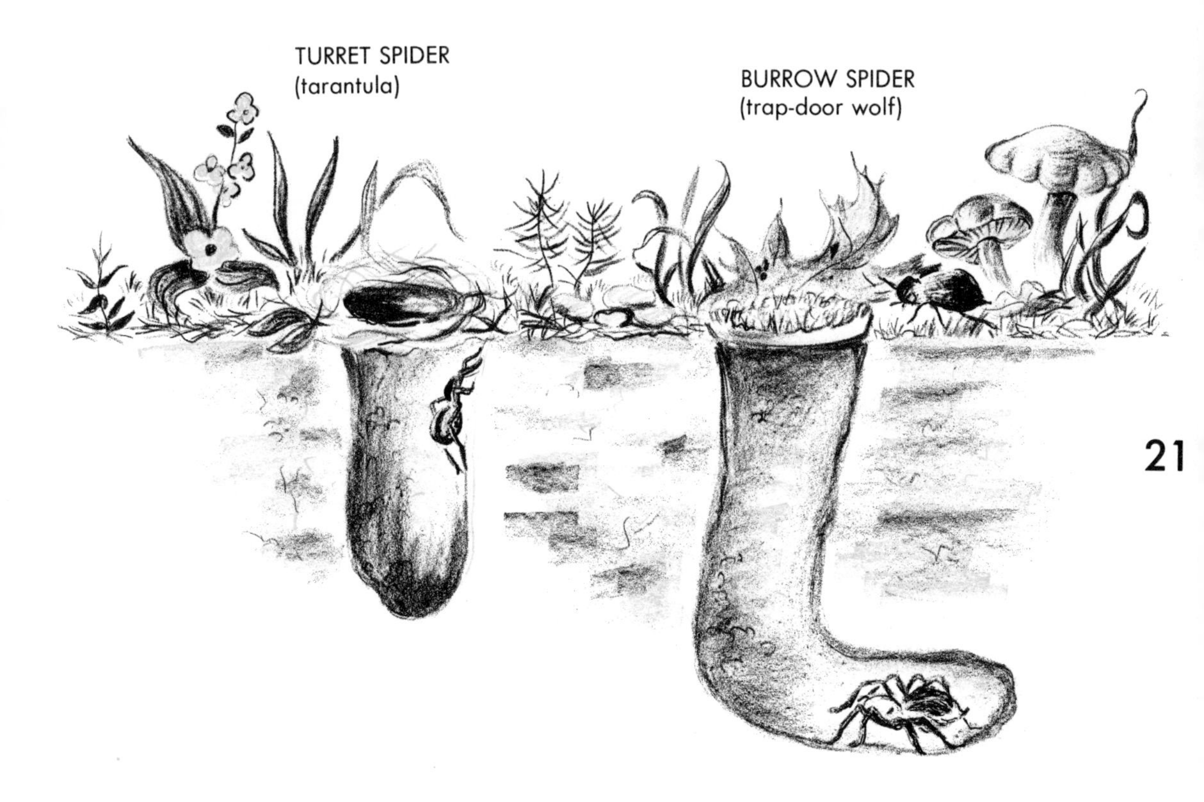

Some spiders live in the ground.

WHAT DO SPIDERS EAT?

Spiders eat other animals.
They eat many insects.
Big spiders can catch tadpoles and even birds.

Spiders eat only insects and other animals which they catch themselves. They do not eat food which other animals catch.

Many spiders catch food in their webs.

A trap-door spider waits for an insect to come along and get caught in its trap.

Some spiders hunt for their food. The wolf spider hunts insects. It goes after an insect when it sees one.

HOW DO SPIDERS MOVE FROM PLACE TO PLACE?

Spiders can run fast with their eight legs. They can run, walk and jump.

You can guess how the jumping spider got its name.

BALLOON SPIDERS

Spiders travel in other ways, too. Some of them spin threads. When there are enough threads, they hang on and are blown through the air by the wind.

HOW DO SPIDERS PROTECT THEMSELVES?

Sometimes spiders run fast to get away from enemies.

When the enemies move fast, too, spiders must protect themselves in other ways.

A tarantula spider may bite its enemy. Sometimes the enemy is paralyzed by the bite and then the spider has a chance to escape.

Some kinds of spiders spin
loose threads to trap their enemies.

Some kinds of mother spiders spin egg cases to protect eggs and young spiders. The outside of the egg case makes it hard for enemies to harm young spiders or eggs.

EGG CASE

The color of some spiders helps them to hide from their enemies.

They are not easily seen.

Scientists call this *protective coloration.*

The house spider sometimes acts as though it is dead when an enemy comes near. We can say it plays possum.

Sometimes an enemy
gets caught in the web
of a spider. The spider
quickly spins a thread
and drops down on it.
When the enemy is gone,
the spider may climb
up the thread to the
web again.

A trap-door spider closes the door and holds it tight until an enemy is gone.

Two spiders may get into a fight. If a spider happens to get into a fight and lose a leg, a new leg will grow back in its place.

HOW ARE SPIDERS HELPFUL TO US?

Most kinds of spiders are very helpful to us. They eat insects which are harmful to us. Some of the insects they eat carry diseases. Some other kinds are harmful to our plants.

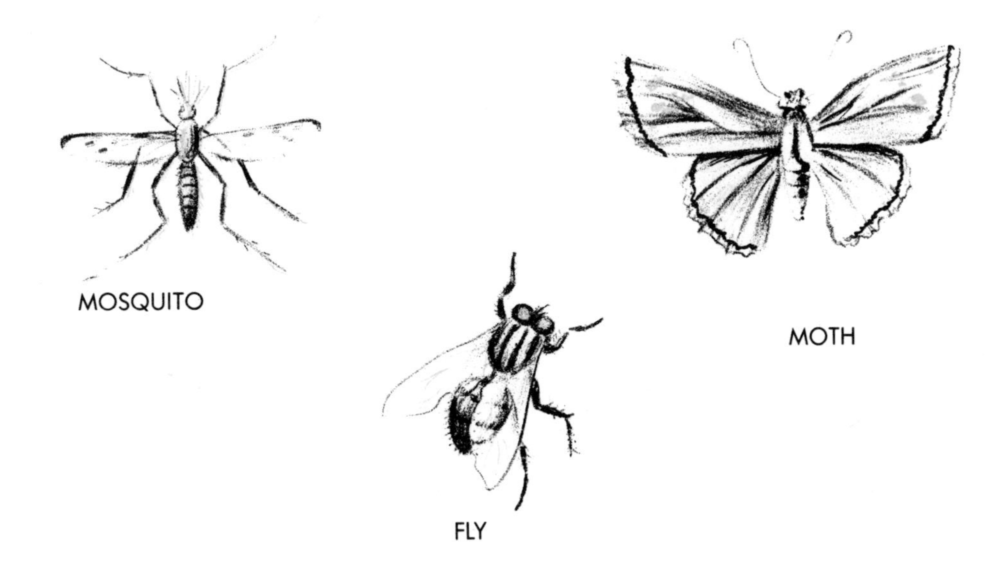

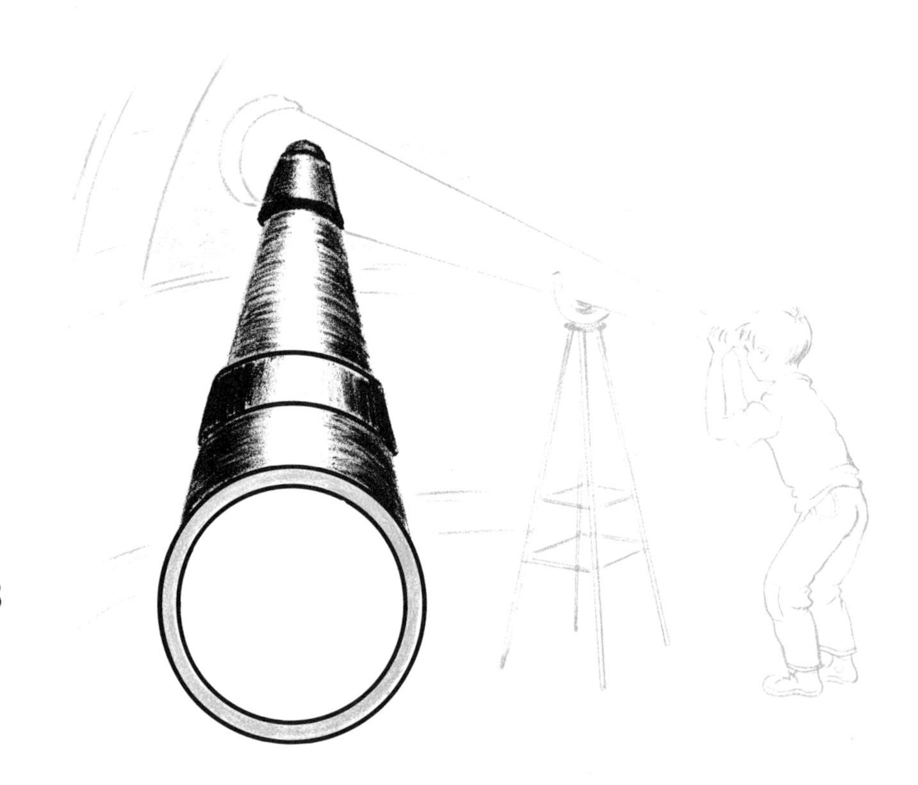

38

The fine silk which spiders spin is useful to us.

It is used in making telescopes.

It is useful because it is so fine and will stretch so much.

HOW ARE SPIDERS HARMFUL TO US?

Sometimes spiders eat insects which are not our enemies. We like to have them eat the harmful ones, but not the helpful ones.

The bite of most spiders is not poisonous. The black widow spider is the only one that would really harm us. It is very poisonous. It is easy to tell a black widow by its hour-glass marking.

WHY ARE SPIDERS SOMETIMES CALLED ENGINEERS?

Spiders are famous for the kinds of webs which they can spin.

Some of the webs are like wheels. We call them *orb* webs. Garden spiders make orb webs.

BANDED GARDEN SPIDER
(orb web)

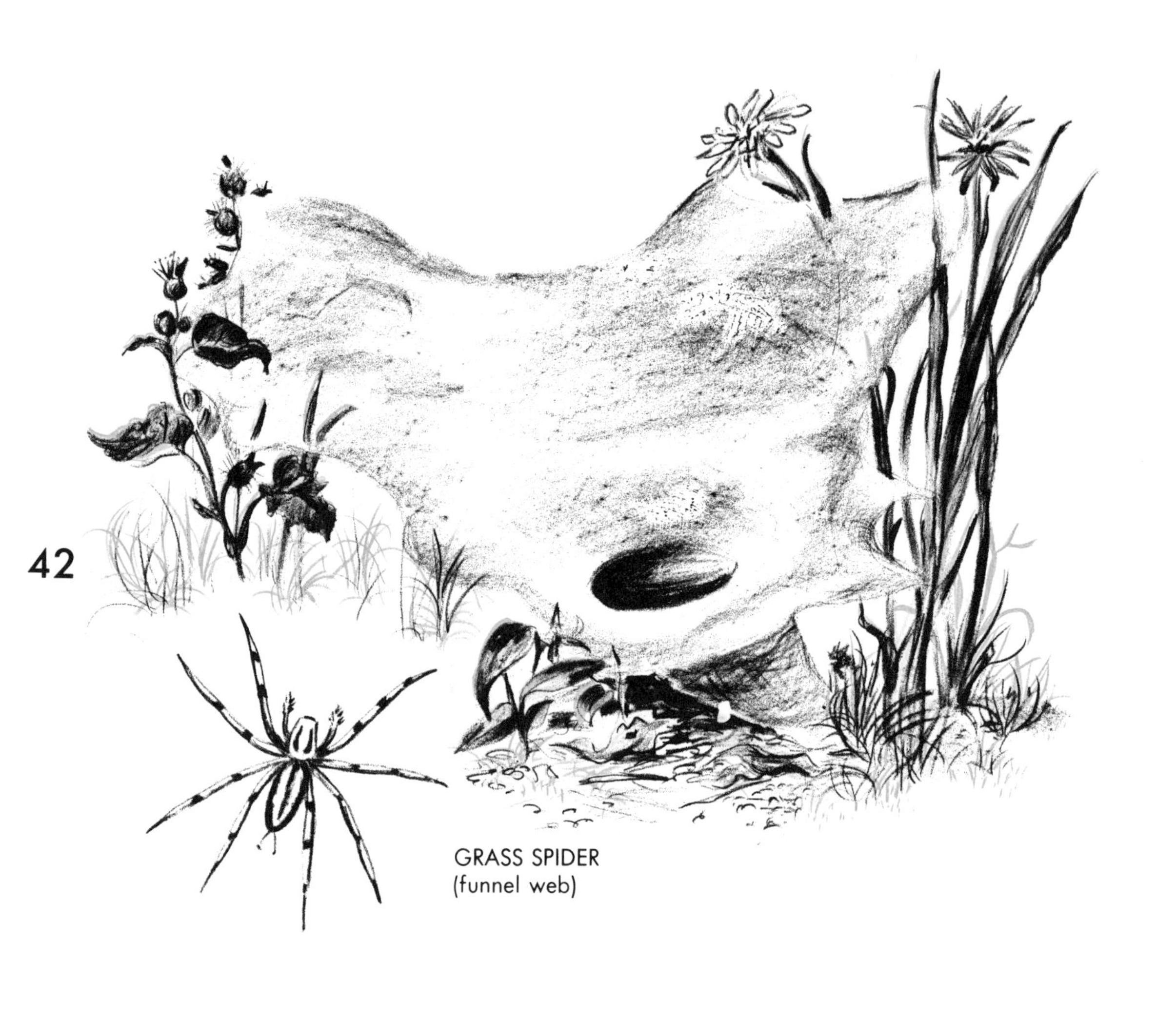

GRASS SPIDER
(funnel web)

A grass spider builds a *funnel* web.

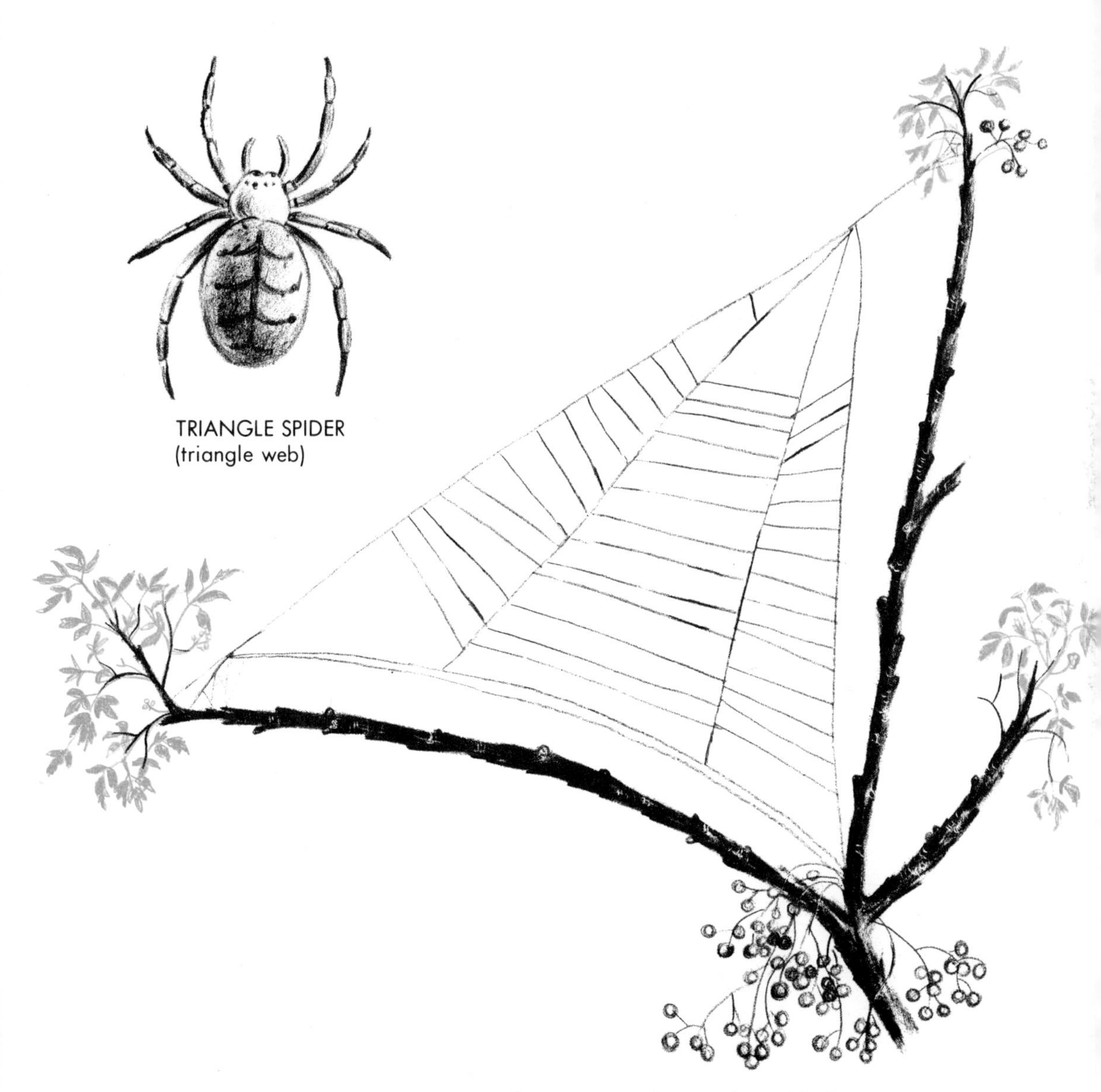
TRIANGLE SPIDER
(triangle web)

A triangle spider builds
a *triangle* web.

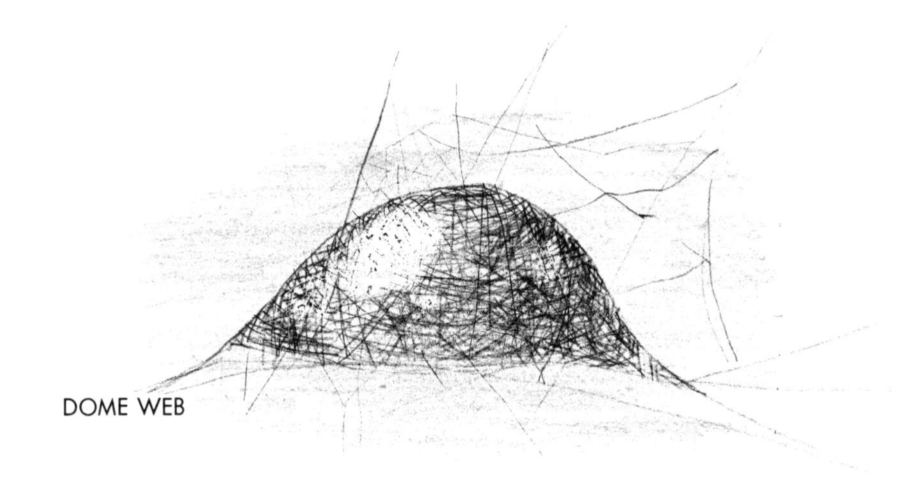

Some spiders make *dome* webs.
Others make *hammock* webs.

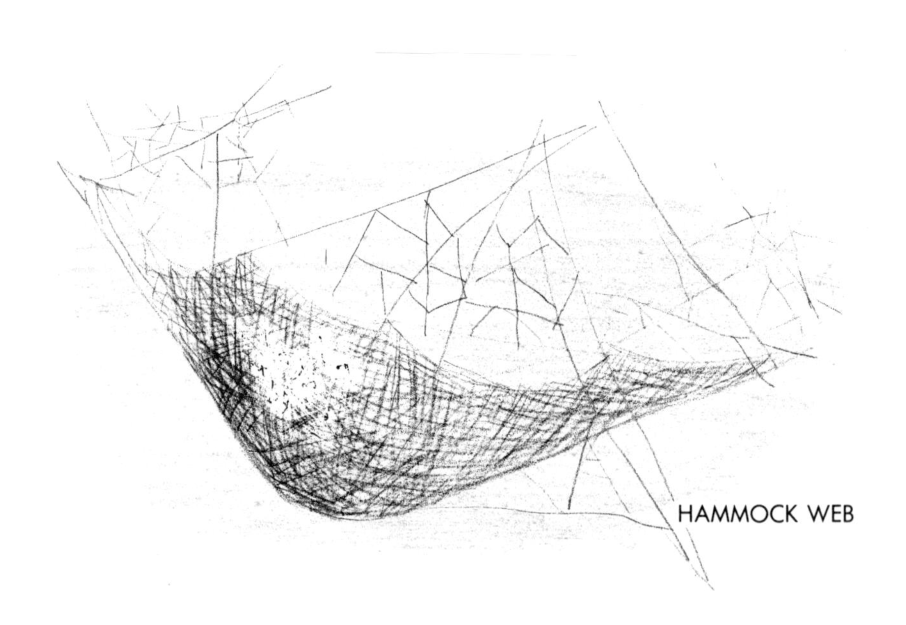

Some spiders build bridges with their silk threads.

A spider uses the silk which it spins for many purposes.

It may make an egg case.

It may use silk threads for traveling.

It may wrap up some of its food in the silk threads.

It may line a home with it.

It may make a food-catching web with silk thread.

This is why spiders are sometimes called engineers.

Do not handle spiders.

Look for them in their natural homes and watch them there. They are most interesting.

I WANT TO KNOW ABOUT. . . . . .
Volume 15
Section B

SCIENCE EXPERIMENTS

By Illa Podendorf

Simple science experiments for beginners have the fascination of magic but, more important, there is the reward of learning simple facts which give a better understanding of the world in which we live.

Illa Podendorf, Laboratory School, University of Chicago, has taught science to beginners. She shares here, with all children, simple experiments that they can do with air, magnets, gravity, water, sound, and heat and cold.

Her approach leads children to find out for themselves by doing and redoing, which is the soundest and most exciting way of learning.

SCIENCE EXPERIMENTS

by Illa Podendorf

pictures by Mary Salem

 CHILDRENS PRESS, CHICAGO

GROLIER ENTERPRISES, CANADA

TABLE OF

CONTENTS

John did some experiments with AIR.

He put a small cloth in the bottom of a large glass.

He turned the glass upside down.

Then he pushed it straight down into the water.

He pulled the glass up and pulled out the cloth. It was dry. He did it again and it was dry.

Do you know why the cloth was dry?

There was air in the glass. Air takes up space. The air did not let the water into the glass.

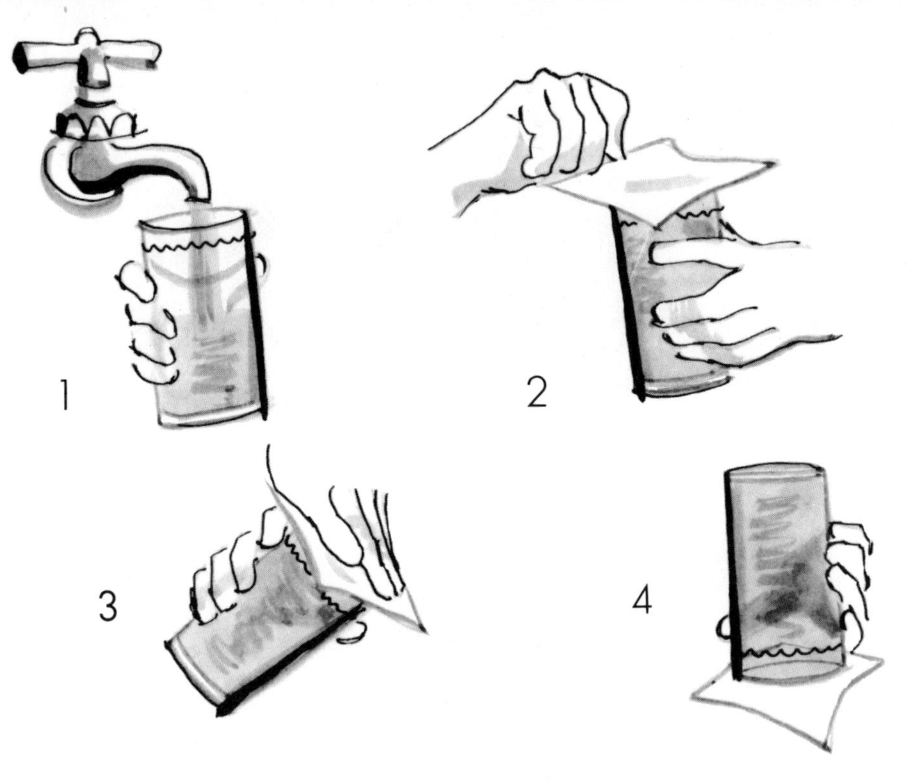

1. John filled a glass with water.
2. He took a piece of paper.
3. He pressed the paper tightly to the top of the glass so that no air could get in.
4. He turned the glass over. Did the water run out? No, the water did not run out.
   Air pushed on the paper and held the water in the glass.

John is carrying some water in a straw. He holds his finger on the top of the straw. You try this. Could you do it?

Air keeps the water from running out of the straw.

John took his finger off the top of the straw. Air got into the top of the straw. The water ran out.

What happened when you took your finger away?

Air pushes up, down, and sideways. Air pushes in all directions.

John got a bottle of water. He put it upside down in a pitcher of water.

He blew air into the bottle.
What do you think happened?
The air pushed out the water.

The bottle had air in it.
John pulled the air out of the bottle.
Water ran in to take the place of the air.
Water went into the bottle because air pushed on the water in the pitcher.

John tried to find a way for the air to push the water out of his fish bowl.

He filled a tube with water.

He pinched the ends of the tube so that no air could get in.

He put one end of the tube in the water in the fish bowl.

He pointed the other end down into an empty pail.

Then he stopped pinching the ends of the tube.

"I have a SIPHON," said John. But it did not work.

He tried again. This time it worked.

John did not let air into the tube this time.

A siphon will not work if there is air in the tube.

It will not work if one end is not lower than the other.

John held an empty balloon
in a glass.
He blew air into the balloon.

He could pick up the glass with the balloon.

The air in the balloon pushed hard on the sides of the glass. The picture shows you how it worked. You try it.

Rubber darts stay on the wall because air pushes them on, and holds them there. They fall off if air gets under them.

John made a weather vane.
These are the things he used:

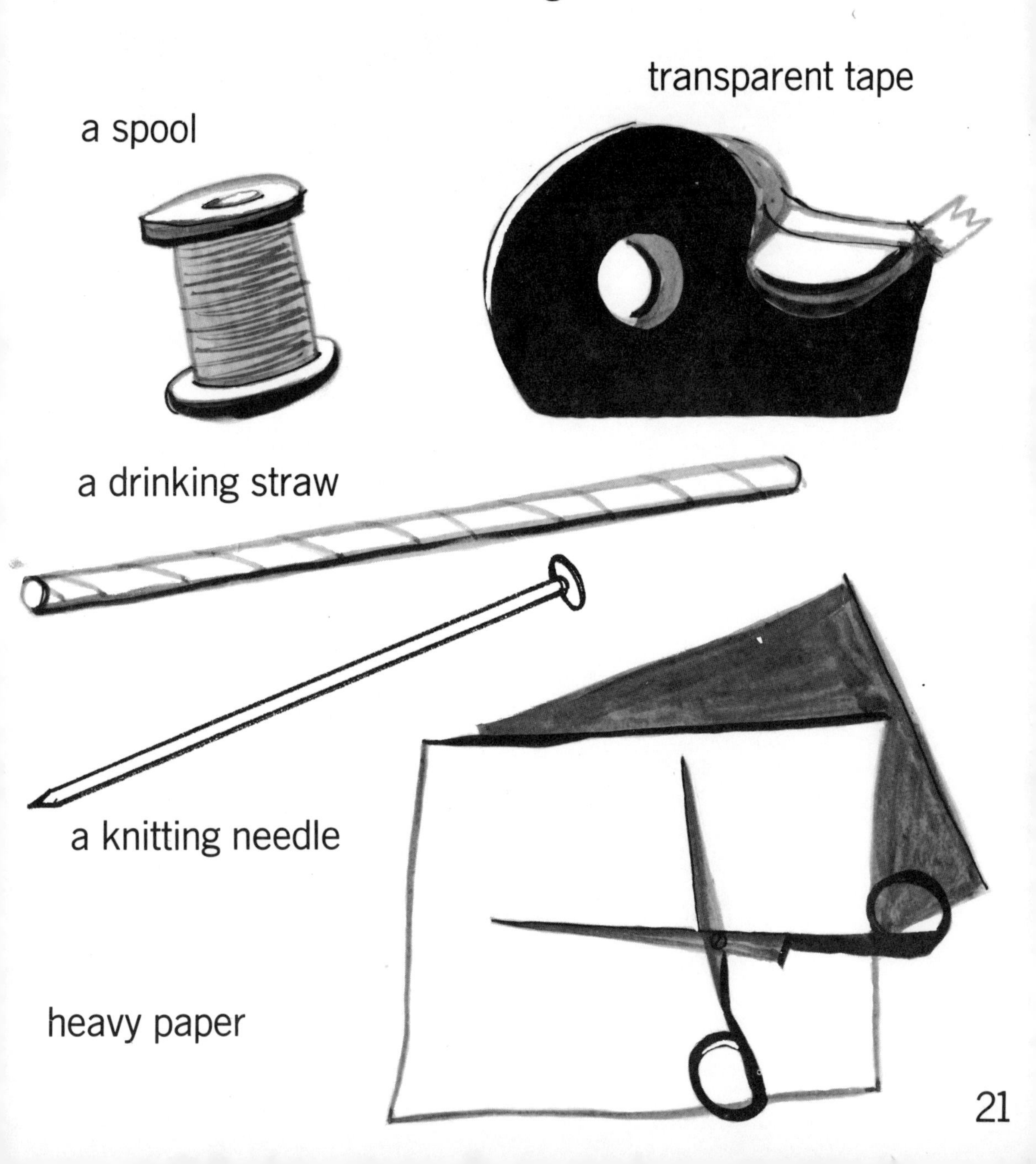

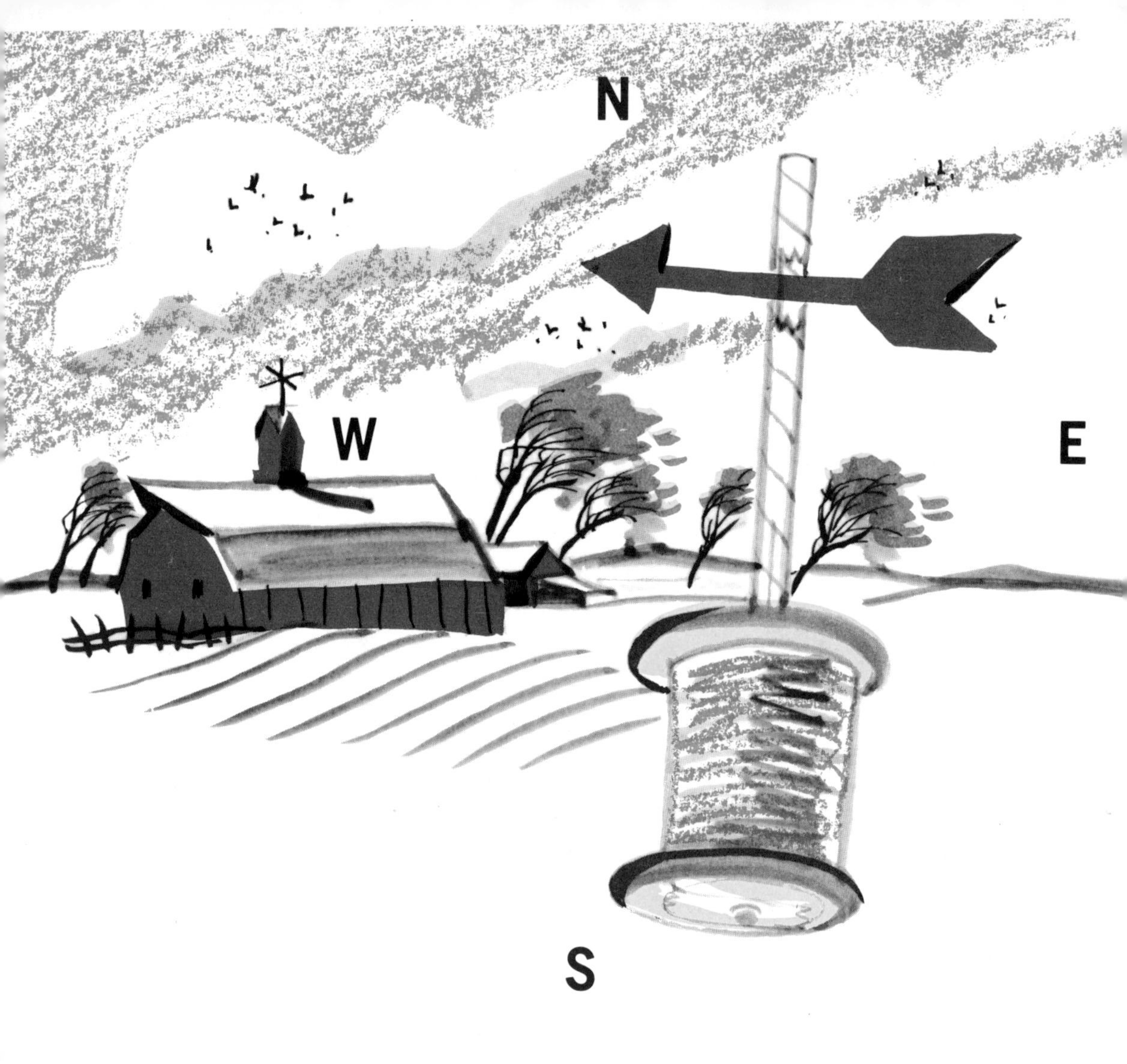

John's weather vane points to the direction from which the wind is coming. What direction is the wind coming from in this picture?

Frank did some
experiments with a MAGNET.

He found that a magnet would not
pick up some of these things.

Do you know which things the
magnet will pick up? The next two
pages will help you.

Frank's magnet would pick up
none of these things.

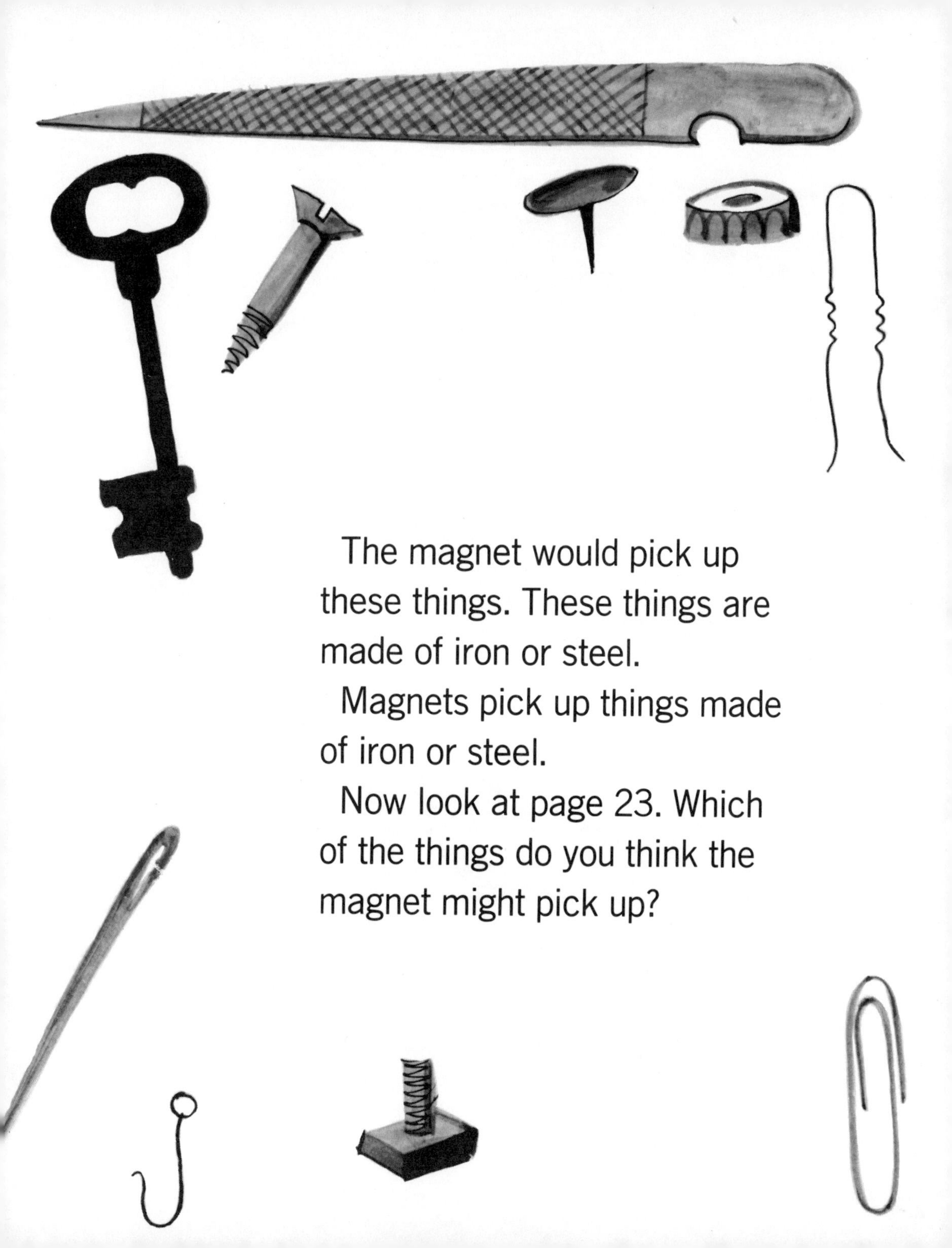

The magnet would pick up these things. These things are made of iron or steel.

Magnets pick up things made of iron or steel.

Now look at page 23. Which of the things do you think the magnet might pick up?

Frank found that his magnet would pull through paper.

It would pull through glass.

Frank could make an iron paper clip walk uphill with his magnet.

Can you tell why the paper clip goes uphill on the glass?

Frank had two magnets.

One end of one magnet would pull toward one end of the other magnet. It would push away from the other end of the other magnet.

The ends of magnets are called POLES. A magnet has a north-seeking pole and a south-seeking pole.

A north-seeking or N pole of one magnet will pull toward a south-seeking or S pole of another magnet.

Two N poles or two S poles will push away from each other.

Magnets come in different shapes. They come in different sizes.

Big magnets are not always the strongest magnets.

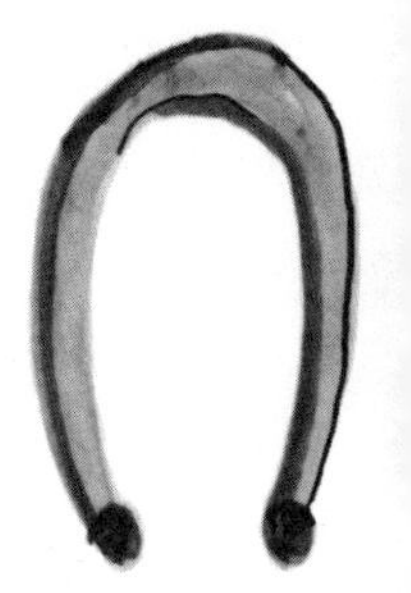

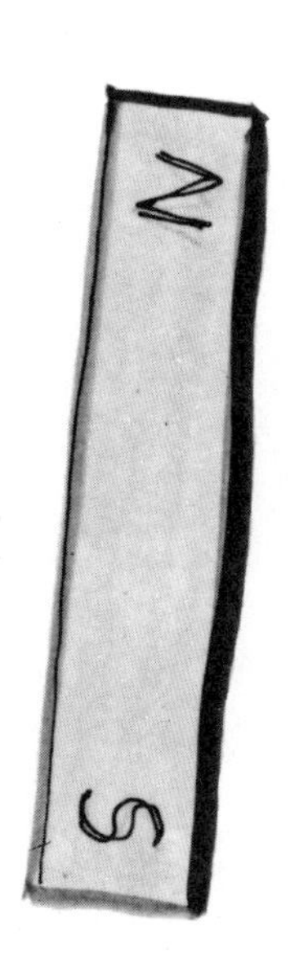

Frank found that a magnet
could make a boat move away.

He turned the magnet around
and the other end made the boat
move toward it.

Do you know why this happened?

Frank made his boat like this:

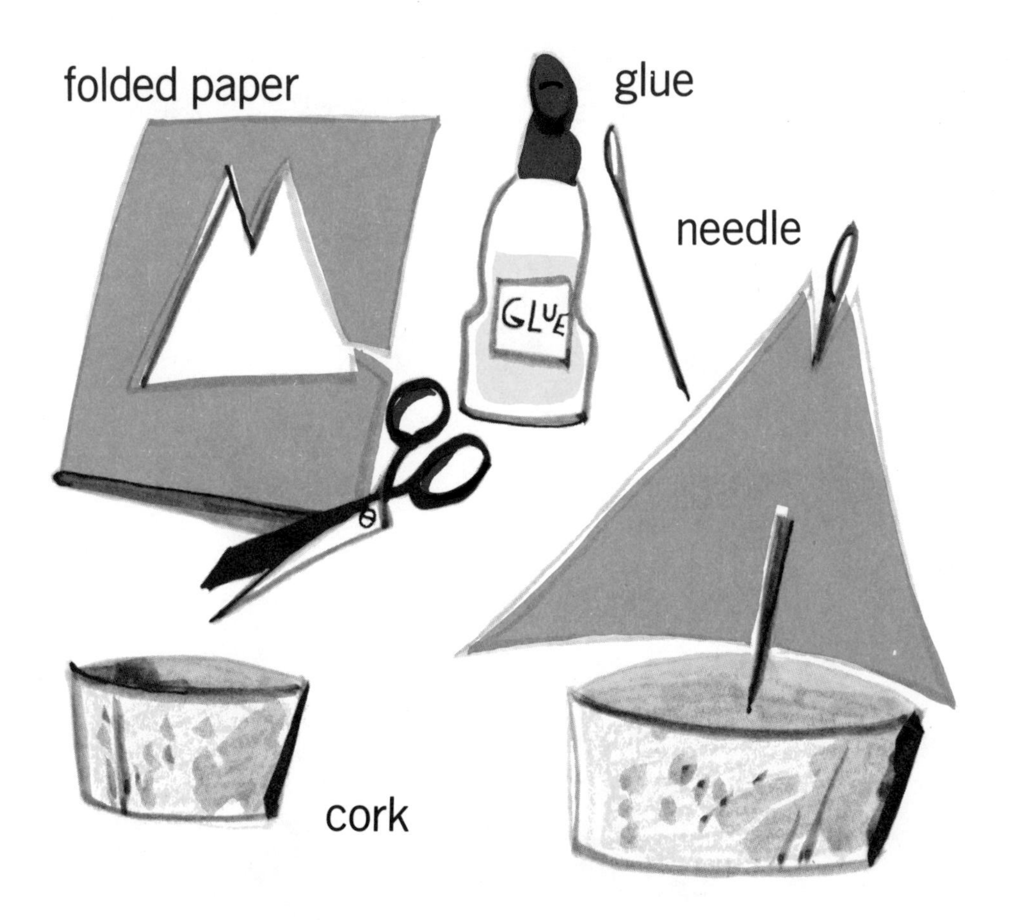

The magnet made the boat move because there was a steel needle in it. The steel needle had an N and an S pole.

Alice did some experiments with GRAVITY.

Gravity is the pull of the earth. Sleds slide downhill
because of the
pull of
gravity.

Alice made a roly-poly toy. She filled half a rubber ball with clay. She put a stick in the middle of the clay.

She made a picture for the top of the stick. The toy would not tip over. It was heaviest where gravity pulls hardest.

Alice put a fork in each side of an apple. Now she could balance it on her finger.

The pull of gravity on the forks helped her balance the apple.

Alice balanced a clothespin doll on her finger.

She used a wire, two keys, and a nail.

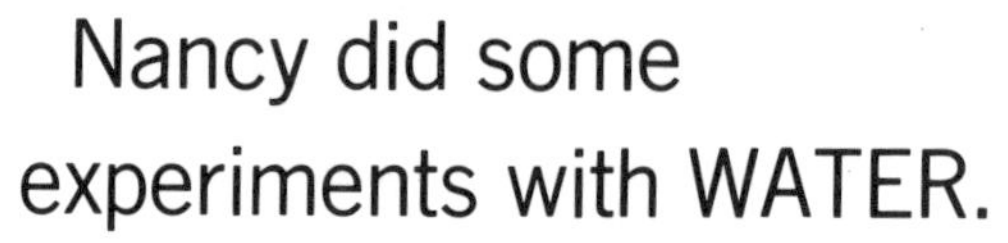

Nancy did some experiments with WATER.

She blew on the water and made waves.

She dropped a penny, a stone, a cork, a feather, and a piece of paper in the water.

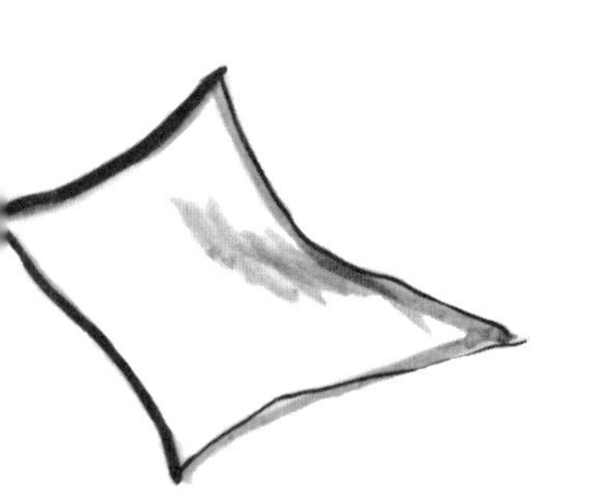

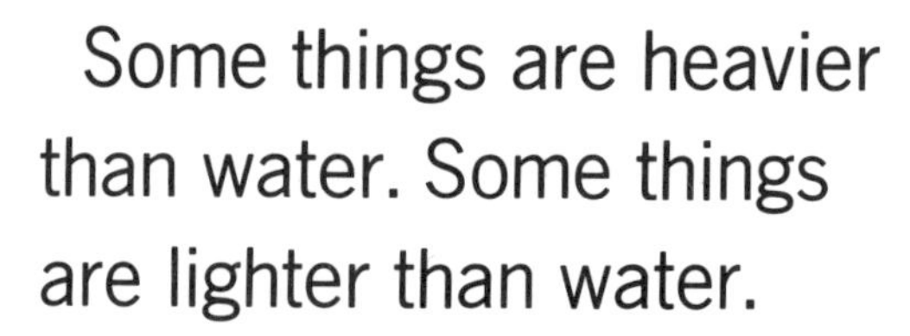

Some things are heavier than water. Some things are lighter than water.

The stone and the penny were heavier than water. They sank to the bottom. The other things stayed on top.

When water disappears into the air, we say it EVAPORATES.

Nancy marked off two places the same size on a blackboard.

She rubbed water on both of them with a wet cloth. She fanned one of them. It dried first. She did this several times.

Always, the one she fanned dried first. Water evaporates faster if there is wind blowing on it.

Nancy took two handkerchiefs the same size. She put them in water. She hung one up straight. She folded the other several times. Then she hung it up. She did this experiment several times. The handkerchiefs she hung up straight dried faster.

Nancy did another experiment with wet handkerchiefs. She hung one of them in the sunshine. She hung the other in the shade.

Always, the one in the sunshine dried first.

Moving air and sunshine help evaporation.

Water is evaporating out of lakes, rivers, and oceans all the time.

Tiny bits of water go into the air.

Someday the tiny bits of water that went into the air will gather together and come down again. Then it will be rain.

Jim did some experiments with SOUND.

He was listening to the radio.

He held his ears back close to his head and listened.

He cupped his hands behind his ears and listened. The sound was much louder when he cupped his hands behind his ears.

Air carries sound waves.

Jim's hands helped to catch the waves. You could try this.

Jim's father's watch was on a table. Jim listened to it with his ear twelve inches, or thirty centimeters, from it. Then he put his ear to the table the same distance from the watch. The watch sounded much louder.

Sound travels better through wood than through air.

Jim and Alice made something that they called a telephone.

They made holes in the bottoms of two small tin cans.

They put the ends of a long string through the holes and tied knots in the ends of the string.

They rubbed wax on the string.

Then they pulled the string tight and talked to each other.

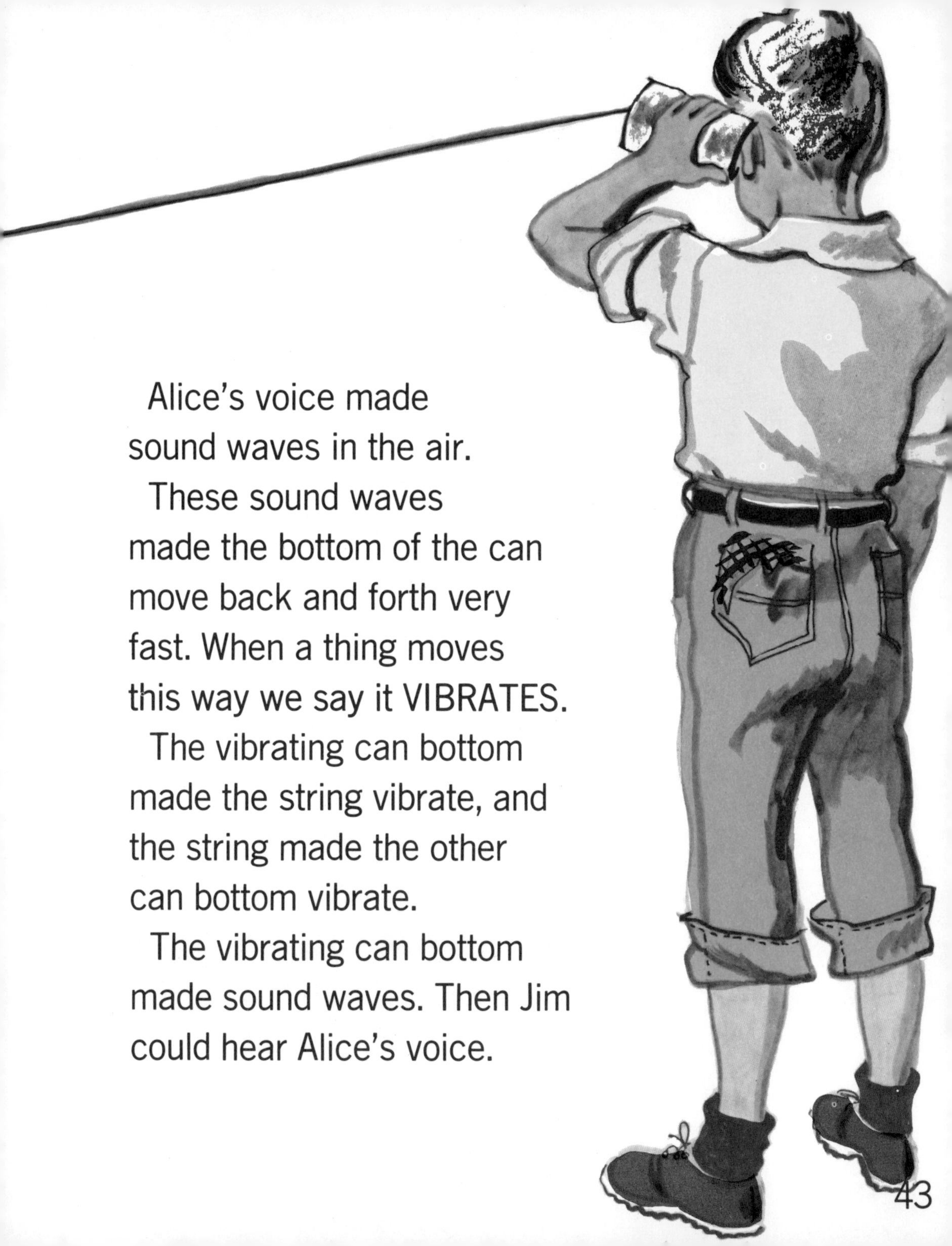

Alice's voice made sound waves in the air.

These sound waves made the bottom of the can move back and forth very fast. When a thing moves this way we say it VIBRATES.

The vibrating can bottom made the string vibrate, and the string made the other can bottom vibrate.

The vibrating can bottom made sound waves. Then Jim could hear Alice's voice.

Robert did some experiments with HEAT and COLD.

He got a trick ball and ring for his birthday.

Sometimes the ball would go through the ring. Sometimes it would not.

When he made the ball very cold, it would go through. When the ball was hot it would not go through.

Can you think of a reason for this? Page 47 will give you an idea.

Robert did another experiment.
He used a bottle with some water in it. Look at the glass tube inside the rubber stopper.

When Robert ran hot water over the bottle, water went up the tube.

When he ran cold water over the bottle, the water came down the tube.

The air in the bottle gets bigger when it is heated. It takes up more space.

THINK ABOUT THESE THINGS:

Air takes up space.

Air pushes on things.

Wind is air moving fast.

Magnets pick up iron and steel.

Magnets pull through paper and glass.

Unlike poles of magnets pull on each other.

Like poles of magnets do not pull on each other.

Gravity is the pull of the earth on all things.

Scales tell us how hard gravity is pulling on us.

Water will evaporate.

Wind helps water to evaporate.

Sunshine helps water to evaporate faster.

Sound travels better through wood than through air.

Heat makes most things get bigger.

Cold makes most things get smaller.

I WANT TO KNOW ABOUT . . . . . .
Volume 15
Section C

TIME

by Feenie Ziner
and Elizabeth Thompson

illustrations by
Katherine Evans

CHILDRENS PRESS, CHICAGO

GROLIER ENTERPRISES, CANADA

How do you know
what time it is?

You can tell
something about time
by looking at the sun.

It is morning at sunrise.

It is noon when the sun is highest in the sky.

It is evening
when the sun sets.

When the sun
shines on the other
side of our round earth,
it is night time
for us.

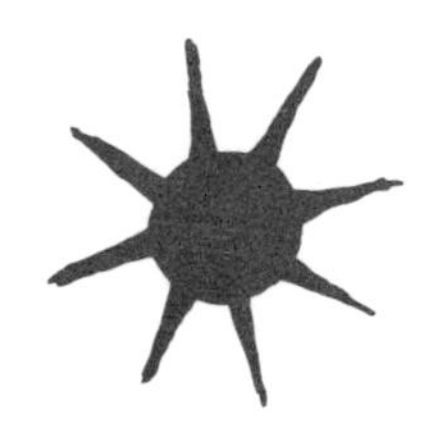

But you cannot count hours just by looking at the sun.

A shadow stick can help us count the hours.

A shadow stick
points straight up.

The stones around the stick mark the hours.

A shadow stick is like a clock.

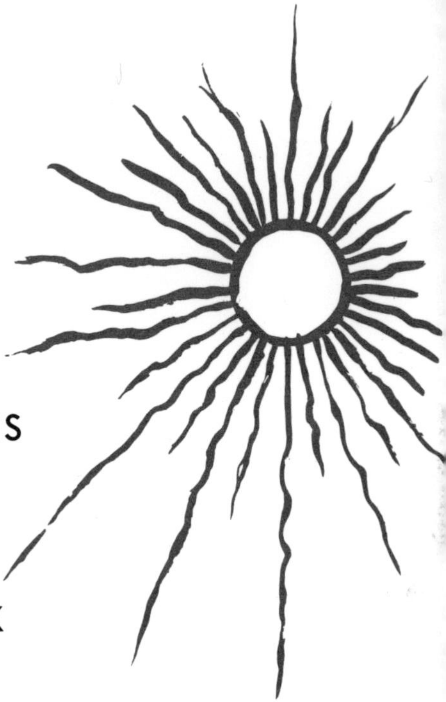

As the earth turns
the sun makes the
shadow of the stick
fall on the stones.

The shadow moves
from one stone to
the next in one hour.

Can you tell time
on a cloudy day
with a shadow stick?

No.

Can you tell time
at night
with a shadow stick?

No.

A sundial is much
like a shadow stick.

There is a way
to tell time
that works both
night and day.

It works
when it is sunny
or cloudy.

It is a candle clock.

A candle clock
is painted with
bands of color.
It takes an
hour for each
band to burn.

If you light
a candle clock
at 8 o'clock
and burn 2 bands,
what time will
it be?

Ten o'clock.

People can
count hours
by burning ropes.

They tie knots
in the rope to
mark the hours.

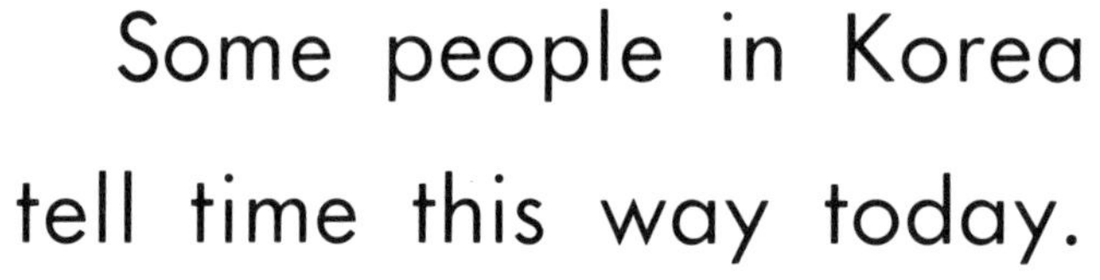

Some people in Korea tell time this way today.

It takes one hour for the rope to burn from one knot to the next.

Candle clocks and rope clocks do not need the sun.

Can the candle clock or the rope clock be used over again? No.

Water clocks
were used in China
long, long ago.

A watchman put
an empty bowl
into a pool
of water.

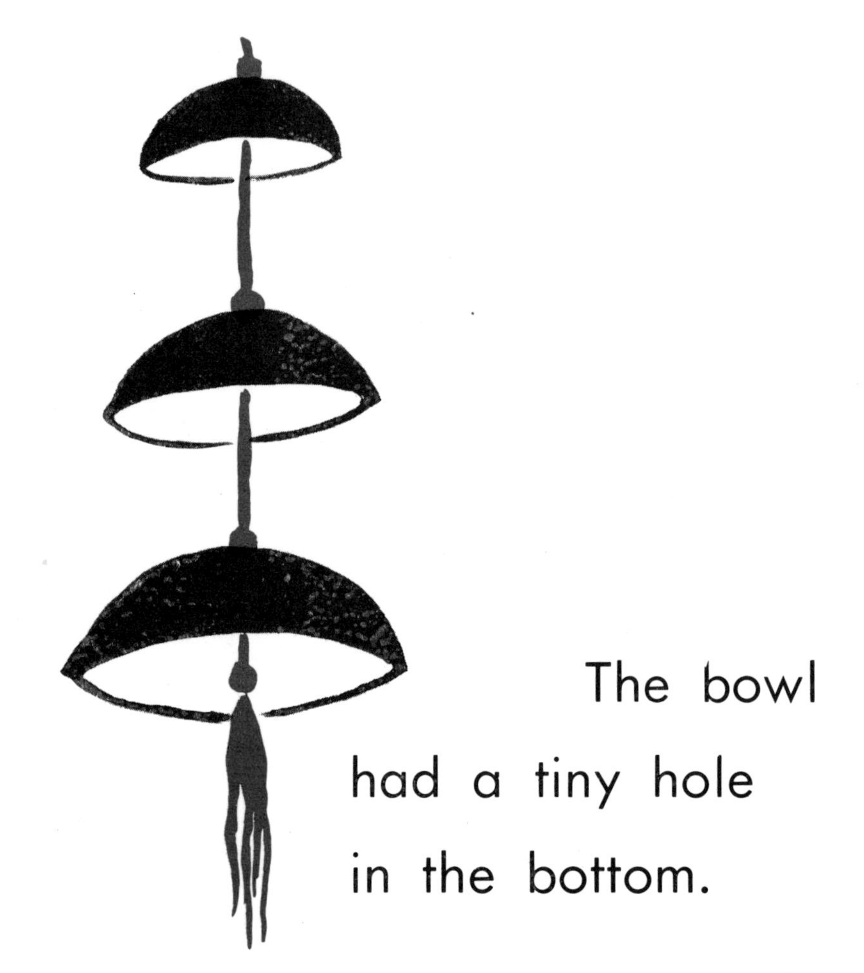

The bowl had a tiny hole in the bottom.

It took one hour for the bowl to fill with water.

It sank to the
bottom of the pool
when it was full.

The watchman
struck a gong

to tell the people that
an hour had passed.

Then he emptied
the bowl and put it
into the pool again.

Another way of telling time is with an hour glass. It has a queer shape.

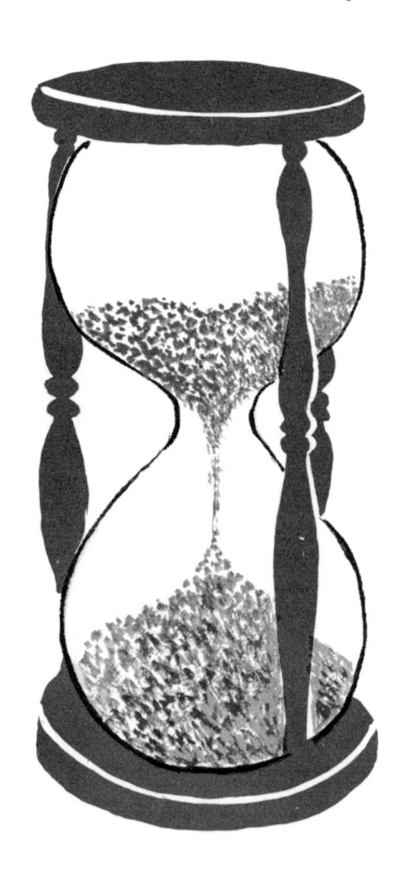

Sand falls from the top
to the bottom.
This takes one hour.

Then the glass is
turned upside down.

An hour glass and a
water clock can be
used again and again.

How do you tell time?

Do you ask your mother, "What time is it?"

Mother looks at the clock.

How does the clock tell
Mother the time?

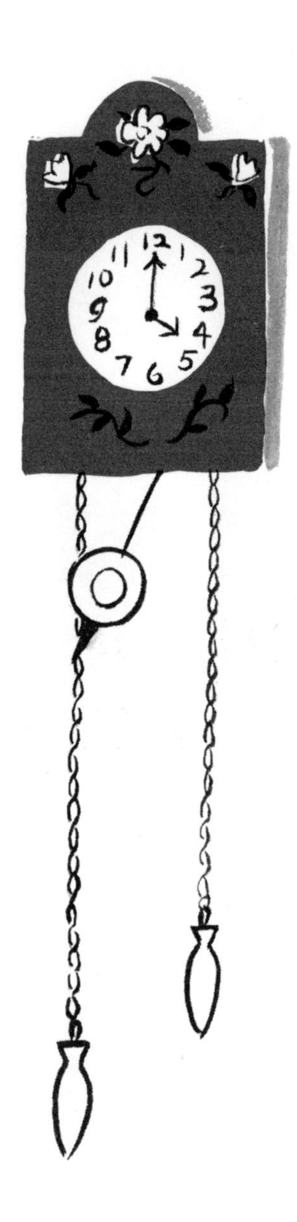

The short hand
points to the
hours.

It takes an hour
for the short hand
to move from one
number to the next.

The short hand points to 12
when the sun is highest in
the sky.

We call that time noon.

The short hand points to 6
at about the time the sun sets.
The short hand moves with the sun.

The long hand points to the minutes.

The long hand goes all around the clock once every hour.

It tells how many minutes after the hour it is.

It takes 5 minutes for the long hand to move from one number to the next.

We count minutes
by fives.

When do you count minutes?

Do you count minutes

when you are not in a hurry?

THINGS TO REMEMBER

The short hand points to the hours.
It takes one hour for the short
hand to move from one number to
the next.
The long hand points to the minutes.
There are five minutes between
each number.
It takes five minutes for the long
hand to move from one number to
the next.
The long hand tells how many
minutes after the hour it is.
The long hand goes all around
the clock while the short hand
is going from one number to
the next.
We count minutes by fives.